> **WARNING:** This eBook is for your personal use only.
>
> You may **NOT** Give Away, Share or Resell
>
> This Intellectual Property in Any Way

All Rights Reserved

Copyright © 2018 – Charles D. Jamieson, Esquire, The Law Firm of Charles D. Jamieson, P.A. All rights are reserved. You may not distribute this report in any way. You may not sell it or reprint any part of it without written consent from the author, except for the inclusion of brief quotations in a review.

Disclaimer

Disclaimer for **"Planning Your Divorce – 9 Important Considerations for Going Your Separate Ways"**

You understand that this book is not legal advice for your divorce or other legal issue. This book is not intended as a substitution for a consultation with an attorney. Requesting this book or viewing the information in it does not create an attorney-client relationship with The Law Firm of Charles D. Jamieson, P.A. or any of its attorneys. To obtain legal advice about your matter, please engage the services of The Law Firm of Charles D. Jamieson, P.A. or another law firm of your choice. To discuss engaging The Law Firm of Charles D. Jamieson, P.A. to help you with your matter, please contact the firm.

THE LAW FIRM OF CHARLES D. JAMIESON, P.A. IS PROVIDING "Planning Your Divorce – 9 Important Considerations for Going Your Separate Ways" (HEREAFTER REFERRED TO AS "BOOK") AND ITS CONTENTS ON AN "AS IS" BASIS AND MAKES NO REPRESENTATIONS OR WARRANTIES OF ANY KIND WITH RESPECT TO THIS BOOK OR ITS CONTENTS. THE LAW FIRM OF CHARLES D. JAMIESON, P.A. DISCLAIMS ALL SUCH REPRESENTATIONS AND WARRANTIES, INCLUDING FOR EXAMPLE WARRANTIES OF MERCHANTABILITY AND FITNESS FOR A PARTICULAR PURPOSE. IN ADDITION, LAW FIRM OF CHARLES D. JAMIESON, P.A. DOES NOT REPRESENT OR WARRANT THAT THE INFORMATION ACCESSIBLE VIA THIS BOOK IS ACCURATE, COMPLETE OR CURRENT.

Except as specifically stated in this book, neither, The Law Firm of Charles D. Jamieson, P.A. nor any authors, contributors, or other representatives will be liable for damages arising out of or in connection with the use of this book. This is a comprehensive limitation of liability that applies to all damages of any kind, including (without limitation) compensatory; direct, indirect or consequential damages; loss of data, income or profit; loss of or damage to property, and claims of third parties and punitive damages.

> *"By failing to prepare, you are preparing to fail."*
> —Benjamin Franklin

> *"Before anything else, preparation is the key to success."*
> —Alexander Graham Bell

"I've written this book to assist individuals to prepare for one of the most significant issues in their lives. Many studies have found divorce to be one of the most emotionally traumatizing events that a person can survive. The most traumatizing event is the death of a spouse or a child. Given that divorce can have significant emotional and financial impacts on one's present life and future existence, it is in everyone's best interest to prepare carefully regarding their divorce. One first step of preparation is educating yourself about the issue of divorce. I believe that in this book you will find important information and suggestions that you should carefully consider when planning your divorce or to consider even when you are in the middle of your divorce. Our office believes that educated clients make the best decisions. With that in mind I invite you to read on ..."

Sincerely,

Charles D. Jamieson, Esquire

The Law Firm of Charles D. Jamieson, P.A.

To schedule a confidential, systematic case evaluation regarding your Florida divorce, please call the Law Offices of Charles D. Jamieson, P.A. at 561-478-0312 or visit us at www.cjamiesonlaw.com.

Copyright © 2018 — Charles D. Jamieson, Esquire – All Rights Reserved Worldwide.

Planning Your Divorce—9 Important Considerations for Going Your Separate Ways   www.cjamiesonlaw.com

TABLE OF CONTENTS

Starting Out 5

Consideration 1: Do you stay or do you go? 8

Consideration 2: Financial Planning and Budgeting 11

    Budgeting 12

Consideration 3: Parenting 14

    TimeSharing and Contact Schedules 15

Consideration 4: Dating is NOT a Good Idea!!! 17

Consideration 5: Avoid Stress and Conflict 18

    Consider Your Health 19

    Diet, Sleep and Exercise 21

    Domestic Violence 22

Consideration 6: Understanding the Cost of Divorce 23

    Legal Fees 24

Consideration 7: FILING for Divorce 25

    Choosing a Good Divorce Lawyer 25

    Initial Consultation 26

    Ask Questions at the Initial Consultation 28

    Rates and Retainers 29

    Controlling Costs 30

To schedule a confidential, systematic case evaluation regarding your Florida divorce, please call the Law Offices of Charles D. Jamieson, P.A. at 561-478-0312 or visit us at www.cjamiesonlaw.com.

Copyright © 2018 — Charles D. Jamieson, Esquire – All Rights Reserved Worldwide.

Other Cost Control Tips 31

Identify Your Team and Documents 32

Petition for Divorce 34

Who Files First? 35

Temporary Support 36

Injunction 37

The Cost to File 37

Consideration 8: Why You Should Consider Getting Divorced in 2018 38

Consideration 9: Collaborative Divorce 41

What's next? 44

STARTING OUT

Divorce stinks. It is as simple as that.

Divorce is a painful, emotionally draining, financially expensive, time consuming, and frustrating experience that will have a long-lasting impact on you and the other members of your family. Divorce will affect your life: financially, emotionally, and will impact the overall quality of life for your future and your family's future.

No one files for divorce on a whim. It may not even be your choice. Over time, you and your spouse will evolve, mature, and approach your life with different perspectives and expectations than those that you possessed when you started your relationship. This is a natural and inevitable result from living with another person. To save a marriage, though, both spouses must be seriously committed. If your marriage is conflicted and you are interested in saving it, you may wish to seek the help of a marriage counselor to attempt to rekindle your marriage and relationship. However, when emotions are heated, a calm, rational discussion between you and your spouse to identify the roots of your marital problems can be impossible to occur. Finding a caring and competent marriage counselor may help you to save your marriage or, at the very least, save you the months or years of dissatisfaction and anguish that can occur if you try to resolve your marriage on your own without the guidance or assistance of professional help.

In the beginning, (even if you don't hire an attorney to handle your separation or divorce), you should obtain as much information as possible about the divorce process before you discuss divorce with your spouse or start a divorce action in court. The purpose of this e-book is to be one such resource. Although a few individuals are able to resolve their divorces with little or no legal advice, there is no denying that divorce statute, case law and procedural rules in Florida and elsewhere are complex, confusing, and at times mystifying. There are many situations when legal advice can be critical to avoid mistakes that can cause you to lose assets, income, and jeopardize your relationship with your children.

An example is the final distribution of marital assets – the final distribution cannot be changed or modified after the divorce is finalized. The earlier you obtain advice from a competent attorney, to help you understand your options, the better. Some early strategic decisions made with the advice and guidance of legal counsel can make a big difference in the outcome of your divorce.

Perhaps the only good thing about divorce is that eventually the process will be over and life will continue. However, what you choose to do during and prior to your divorce can have huge consequences. Be on guard against your emotional responses to your divorce. Separate the legal aspects and issues from your emotional response. Emotions and memories fade and change over time, while legal judgments persist. Feelings often associated with divorce include "failure," "guilt," "anger," "frustration," and "fear." These feelings can fade and evolve over time. They do not need to define you. Empower yourself to deal with these feelings by educating yourself on the issues, options, process, and consequences of divorce.

Before the beginning of your divorce case is the best time to educate yourself and prioritize your specific goals. At first, you may just have some vague ideas. Over time, you will begin to know what you want for yourself and your children.

This e-book does not begin to address all the issues, and fact patterns that can often occur during a Florida divorce case. It is an invitation, a first step, and should be used as a companion to other resources such as www.cjamiesonlaw.com (where you can find our blogs and other sources of information). Also, review additional videos on our YouTube channel at Charles D. Jamieson P.A. https://www.youtube.com/channel. And, there is just no substitute for obtaining the advice and services of an expert family law attorney.

At our family law firm, we believe all people are unique and that there is no such thing as a cookie cutter "one size fits all" approach to divorce. We also have seen the financial and emotional destruction that occurs in many divorces. Our objective is to make you aware that there are a number of alternatives that fit your unique situation. By educating yourself about the considerations for divorce that follow, we hope to help you create the kind of results in your divorce that minimize the financial and emotional costs to your life, and lead to a more successful future for you and your children.

Also keep in mind that while we present options and strategies... they often only make up half the equation. For each of these considerations discussed in this book, there are corresponding experts (financial, psychology, and legal) who are available to help guide you. The best approach is often built around the concept of assembling a support "team." Often your attorney is going to be your best source for referrals and recommendations of knowledgeable, passionate, experienced family law professionals who understand divorce/family law and your needs.

We encourage you to read, learn and prioritize your goals, while building your team, as you approach this difficult life experience.

CONSIDERATION 1: DO YOU STAY OR DO YOU GO?

"Should I stay or should I go now?
Should I stay or should I go now?
If I go there will be trouble
And if I stay it will be double
So, come on and let me know"

The Clash

Should I Stay or Should I Go? Lyrics

Don't feel that you must leave your marital home just because your spouse asks you to leave. Do not move out of the family home until after you have consulted with an experienced Florida lawyer. Even if you have agreed with your spouse to move out, by doing so, you may lose the use of the house, access to the equity, and it could result in the loss of parenting time with your children. Seeking experienced legal advice prior to leaving the home may protect your rights and allow you to move out when it is reasonable and advantageous for you to do so. However, if you believe you or your children are in danger – you should consider vacating your home, finding a safe place, and immediately contacting the police and an attorney.

Leaving the family home may reduce some immediate stress today, but it may create additional stress in the near future. Understand that leaving the family home could be misinterpreted and communicate a position that you, in fact, are not taking. Setting reasonable expectations early on with your spouse may help avoid an adversarial divorce or a legal dispute over who will continue to reside in the marital home.

Consider your finances, and if you leave also consider what your continued contribution of household expenses for the marital residence may be. You may be required to pay a portion or all of the expenses for the marital home even though you do not live there anymore. Understand that divorce has a negative economic impact on both spouses and continued payment of the costs to maintain the marital residence may be a shared expense. Staying under the same roof as your spouse offers a unique opportunity to share everyday expenses more efficiently until an agreement is reached or final judgment is granted. Courts may also consider whether the spouse who resides in the marital residence, can afford to pay all of its expenses. However, always remember that the departing spouse may be required to contribute to the marital residence's expenses.

Before leaving the family home, you should talk to your Florida Board Certified Marital and Family Law attorney. If you leave the family residence while the divorce is still pending, it can impact other unresolved legal issues, such as parenting time, and spousal support/alimony. Remember also, that this interim period between the commencement and conclusion of your divorce, can be used to negotiate, adjust to, and foster a parenting plan that is acceptable to both spouses.

Prior to the start of your divorce, gather documents and financial information. Gather all financial information and documents to which you have access and make copies of documents that might easily be destroyed or lost. Such important legal documents including copies of vehicle titles, mortgage statements, bank statements, insurance policies, receipts of large purchases (i.e. artwork), investment/retirement accounts, and include debts (such as credit lines, credit cards, and personal loans/liabilities). Record these financial documents and information in a detailed list or inventory. Having an organized, detailed list will save you time and money. Also, include photographs or video recordings of your home, furnishings and personal belongings and note the condition and needed repairs, if any. Store all of this information in a safe location, outside of the home, and located where your spouse does not have access.

If you want to stay, can your spouse force you to leave from the marital home? Neither spouse can force the other to leave – there is an exception for domestic abuse, where the court can order a spouse to leave. To minimize the chances of the court issuing an order essentially evicting you from the marital home, avoid confrontations with your spouse. During the stress of a divorce, small complaints and criticisms can escalate quickly, even to physical assaults or threats. Handle contested issues and negotiations through your attorney. They will be able to determine what is important to the outcome of the divorce. Do not issue threats of any kind – or respond to any threats made by your spouse. Instead walk away. Something as simple as blocking someone's egress from a room could be considered abusive. If you appear to be the initiator of domestic violence, even if you were not (especially in the case of abuse), it can have a negative impact on your divorce and/or access to your children. However, if you believe you or your children are in danger, you should find a safe place and immediately contact the police and an attorney. If violence or serious threats do occur, call the police immediately.

Regardless of whether you stay or go, you need to take control of your communication devices and accounts. Cellphones, tablets, laptops, emails, and social media accounts provide incredibly convenient methods to communicate with the world. However, they create a virtual record of our communications and activities. Social media conversations and postings can be used as evidence against you, so you should suspend all social media activities until after your divorce is final. Create a new e-mail account, limited to only communicating with your lawyer. A Gmail account is easy to create and access through a browser. Do not setup the email account through software such as Microsoft Outlook. However, be aware that all email services store copies of messages, even when you are offline. Obtain a different cell phone account separate from any family plan, and reset all

voice mail, email, and social media passwords. In general, do not use any personal computer for which you do not have exclusive administrator rights and a password known only to you. Assume that anything you say or write is being recorded or will be used in court. Be very careful about your communications with your spouse. Assume all of your communications can be used against you in court.

Taking these steps may seem difficult (while you are protecting your communications and your privacy) and may make you feel less connected to the world. Nevertheless, prior to your divorce and during your divorce is an important time to maintain or regain contact with significant people in your life. Let people who care about you know what is going on. You may feel ashamed or embarrassed about your divorce but, these are normal emotions during a divorce and these frustrations are exactly why you should reach out for support. In most communities, you will be able to find divorce support groups. Take advantage of the support that is available to you from family, friends, neighbors, or support groups.

While you remain in the home, you need to establish boundaries or rules with your spouse, partly in preparation for when you leave the home and also so that you can't be accused of sending mixed signals. This is true especially if the decision to get divorced is not mutual. Normal routines need to be altered; avoid sleeping in the same room and do not have sexual relations with your spouse. Having sexual relations with a spouse, especially one who has cheated, can be used as an argument that you have condoned the cheating and forgiven your spouse. And while Florida is a "no fault" divorce state, adultery can impact custody/visitation, equitable distribution of assets, alimony, and other issues.

CONSIDERATION 2: FINANCIAL PLANNING AND BUDGETING

Financial planning and budgeting prior to, and during, a divorce is so important. Yet, let's face it, many of us just don't like doing these tasks. One way to increase your chances of completing this important task is to consider working as early as possible with a professional in the beginning, rather than in the middle of your divorce. Hiring a professional can reduce the overall cost of your divorce, both in time and money. It is quite possibly one of the most important actions you will make in your divorce. An experienced Florida Board Certified Marital and Family Law attorney will be able refer you to financial professionals who specialize in divorce forensic analysis and/or divorce financial planning.

Consider the course or direction that your divorce will take: Contested divorces will require larger budgets since there will be litigation expenses. In contrast, collaborative law divorces result in faster, less expensive, less acrimonious divorce proceedings. It is recommended that you seek financial divorce advice prior to starting any divorce process.

Run a credit report on yourself. Also, sign up for a credit monitoring service during the course of your divorce.

Establish and maintain a separate bank account to which only you have access. Deposit your earnings into that account. Make all automatic deposits into this account but remember that you may still be responsible for the joint expenses of the marital residence and other ordinary expenses from your marriage.

Ensure that all bills are being paid, regardless of which spouse's name is on the account.

Do not threaten to cause undue financial duress or attempt to financially damage the other spouse or your family by quitting your job, selling assets at a "fire sale," making large purchases, refusing to pay a shared bill, or making new binding investments. These behaviors are never looked upon favorably by the courts.

Put money aside and prepare to be responsible paying at least initially, your own legal fees, expert fees, and court costs. Depending on your financial circumstances you also may be responsible for all or a portion your spouse's legal costs, regardless of who files the Petition for Dissolution of Marriage.

Close joint credit accounts. Consider requesting a credit limit increase on your credit cards and lines of credit.

Establish your own individual post office box. It can be used for all personal bills and correspondence from your lawyer and other family law professionals, if email is not available to you.

If you need temporary support, you can file for divorce and ask the court to order your spouse to provide temporary spousal support/alimony, child support, attorney fees, timesharing (custody/visitation), and other issues until your divorce is finalized. This is called *pendente lite relief* or temporary relief.

A durable power of attorney is often used in estate planning and wills. If you have previously given your spouse any of these powers, your spouse unilaterally may be allowed to act on your behalf in many legal and financial situations. You do not want your spouse to have this authority if your marriage is disintegrating and/or you are considering filing for a divorce. (They also can liquidate any of your assets and liabilities in your name.) You need to revoke the powers authorized in any such document. Consult with your attorney how to revoke any such documents.

BUDGETING

It is essential that you create a budget. Budgets are often a part of the divorce process and courts will require a budget anytime spousal support or alimony is being requested and, let's face it, having a detailed budget will help you make smarter decisions.

There are many resources available to help you build a budget. Dave Ramsey is a well-known author and radio talk show host who has helped many in your same position. His book, Total Money Makeover, is a great resource for guidance on planning and building a budget – www.daveramsey.com. Other online resources include www.mint.com which will allow you to build detailed budgets for free and electronically connect to checking, savings and investment accounts – you can quickly build a picture of how you are spending and saving your money.

The basic steps in building a budget are quite simple. Start with your income: What are your sources of earned income and your spouse's income? Assemble and document your income sources (paystubs, W-2's, 1099s, R1 forms, bank statements, tax returns, etc.) and make copies. Your lawyer will need them. Next, list expenses: mortgage, utilities, groceries, etc. Document the expenses as well. Finally, subtract monthly expenses from monthly income and identify surpluses, investment accounts, and savings. Be thorough. It is easy to move quickly and forget something. The documentation will be the key later in the divorce process.

The more detailed budget you prepare, the better an understanding you will have of your needs and resources. Later on, your lawyer or finance professional will transform your budget into a Financial Affidavit. The goal for now is to understand how much money it takes for you and your children to live and how much you will need to receive from your spouse. Simply put, having a detailed budget in the beginning will help you make wiser decisions, and often will help obtain the financial relief and a much fairer result. Your budget and financial affidavit will be the most important information you will provide to your attorney and to the court during the divorce.

CONSIDERATION 3: PARENTING

Children often become the innocent and unwilling participants in a divorce. Some parents may believe that a divorce will reduce stress on their children by removing them from the effects of an often-unhealthy relationship with a spouse. Children, even adult children, idealize their parents and their relationship with mom and dad is the most important one in their life. Consequently, it is very important to remain neutral in how you speak about the other parent when your children are present, and to neither defend yourself nor attack (put down) the other parent.

Acting in this way is not easy. Remaining neutral or positive about your spouse (when your emotions are running high), and you possibly feel hurt or anger towards your spouse. It can seem impossible when hurtful or provocative statements are being directed towards you by your spouse – possibly through your own children. Trying to control or influence the other spouse to be a better parent or more cooperative during the divorce is rarely successful. Resist the temptation, and work on yourself and for the best interests of your children. Sometimes good management of your emotions may include communicating through a third party (attorney, counselor, mediator, or friend) to prevent arguments and promote proper communication.

It is fair to say that no one can clearly predict what you will be going through during your divorce, but it also is fair to assume that you are responsible for managing your own feelings. You need to separate your role as a parent from your role as a divorcing spouse. In marriage, we often combine the roles of parent and spouse. But during a divorce, the opposite occurs. Maintaining your self-control and the ability to act and react in a centered fashion instead of being judgmental or resentful is difficult but necessary. For your best interest, and the best interest of your children.

Prior to, and during your divorce, you should keep a parenting journal and a detailed calendar. Use these resources to record events and time spent with your children and, likewise, the events and time your children spend with your spouse. Don't use these resources to record your feelings or thoughts towards your spouse (an example of what not to include in your journal is: "The Loser was nowhere to be seen at Bobby's baseball game…AGAIN!) Your journal and/or parenting calendar could be used in court as a contemporaneous record of what occurred, or to refresh your recollection. Flippant or sarcastic comments go to your credibility and could possibly damage your position.

You also can use the journal and calendar as a way to plan timesharing (visitation) schedules. Consider both parents' work schedules, especially if a spouse will be returning to work. Also, consider things such as school, daycare, transportation, sports, holidays, and doctor's visits. Having a well recorded and thought-out plan is important, it can be used to help prepare and determine the proper timesharing and contact schedule.

TIMESHARING AND CONTACT SCHEDULES

Florida Statutes now use the term "timesharing" instead of "child custody" or "primary residency," and the term "contact schedule" instead of "visitation". No matter what terms you use, the following must be carefully analyzed and considered.

You need to decide if you want to maximize the amount of parenting time and involvement you have with your children and how you will attempt to do so. Where you reside, your work schedule, and where your child lives and attends school, will impact the amount of timesharing you will have with your children. Recent research supports that children can form strong attachments to a number of adults. While the scientific knowledge regarding timesharing has progressed, often societal conventions and the court system have lagged behind… thus the importance of keeping the parenting journal and calendar just mentioned, especially during the commencement of the divorce process. Maximizing your child contact (visitation) schedule is beneficial for both you and your children. Do not let yourself fall into a visitation routine without considering how you might maximize your parenting time.

If you move out of the marital home, work at obtaining the desired schedule as soon as possible. If the parents can't agree on a timesharing and contact schedule, either spouse may ask the court for a temporary timesharing schedule and contact plan for the period during which the divorce is pending. The "status quo" that is established early on is, thus, vitally important later in the process a judge is likely to favor the least amount of disruption to the child's routine.

Furthermore, remember that, no matter how well or poorly that the divorce proceeds, you must do your very best to stay involved with your children. If you can't visit them, call them. Use FaceTime or

Skype to have video calls with your kids. Do whatever it takes to keep in touch, even if it's just a five-minute phone call before bedtime. Tell your children you love them and give them a chance to talk to you. And remember to maintain your neutrality and do not speak negatively about your spouse to your children. Do not use your children to communication with your spouse. Do not discuss the issues of the divorce with your children. Let your children be children and make sure that you act like an adult.

CONSIDERATION 4: DATING IS NOT A GOOD IDEA!!!

Do not date during your divorce. Without doubt this is one of the most common-sense forms of legal and practical advice for divorce clients, yet it is consistently ignored. Perhaps it is ignored since the marriage is already coming to end, and what harm could there be?

A new romantic relationship during your divorce, in some fashion, almost always will impact your divorce negatively. Do not begin a new relationship during your divorce. If you have started a new relationship, you should put it on hold until the divorce has become final. If you have been involved in any extramarital affairs, talk to a lawyer before discussing the extramarital affair with your spouse or anyone else. It is highly likely that your new relationship will be dragged into the divorce process whether it is ultimately settled or litigated since new relationships will raise issues regarding the use and distribution of marital assets, as well as concerns regarding your children and your ability to parent them. Regardless of your feelings, it is not worth it!

Every choice you make will be subject to scrutiny by courts, especially when children are involved. The courts expect parents to make their children their highest priority. Extramarital relationships are never viewed as putting children first. In general, do not introduce your children to new relationships or new romances during the divorce, even if those relationships are just new friends of the opposite sex, platonic or otherwise. Even if your children are teenagers, your new relationships will be too confusing, unfamiliar and unsettling to them especially during and immediately after the divorce. Instead, keep the focus on your family and on the best interest of your children.

If you choose to ignore this advice, be prepared that your paramour is likely to be subjected to some form of scrutiny. They may be called upon to testify or have their deposition taken. Their lives will be put under examination and prior convictions, awkward photos posted on social media, debts under collection, and the slightest aberrations of their lives may end up being scrutinized and entered into the public record of your divorce. Perception and attitude matter even though Florida is a no-fault divorce state.

If you have already started a relationship before you read this, your situation is not unusual. You are not the first, and you will certainly not be the last. But immediately tell your lawyer about it. Talk it through. Don't let your lawyer find out about the relationship later from your spouse's lawyer, or during the middle of a hearing. You'll need to make some tough decisions during your divorce. Just make sure that the decisions you make are informed ones and that they are in the best interest of your children.

CONSIDERATION 5: AVOID STRESS AND CONFLICT

Avoiding stress and conflict seem like odd advice when you are heading straight onto the emotional rollercoaster of divorce… nevertheless, there are actions you can take to minimize stress and conflict during divorce.

Understanding the needs and motives of your spouse is a good place to start. Not understanding or mismatching your approach to divorce against your spouse can cause massive stress. Most likely your divorce can fall into one of three types: 1) Businesslike – Both spouses recognize the marriage is at an end and want to tie off all loose ends; 2) The Amicable Divorce - You will likely remain friends and share parenting comfortably (even with future spouses); and 3) The High Conflict Divorce – You will contest virtually every aspect of your divorce, either as a matter of control or survival. Often your divorce will be some combination of all three.

For businesslike and more amicable divorces, there are alternatives to the stresses and conflicts associated with traditional litigated divorce. Increasingly popular, collaborative family law is an innovative, non-adversarial, method of handling family law matters, including divorces. Collaborative divorce in Florida offers a less adversarial, more private, shorter, and often less expensive method for marriage dissolution, especially when compared to litigation. The collaborative approach requires both parties and their individual attorneys to resolve all issues of the divorce by negotiated agreement. If either side resorts to litigation during the divorce, then the attorneys, mental health professionals, and financial professionals are disqualified and must withdraw from the case. Emphasizing cooperation and interest based on problem-solving strategies (rather than adversarial approaches and litigation), collaborative divorce avoids the destructive position-based arguments associated with other more adversarial approaches. Negotiations between the parties and their lawyers are needs (interest) based. This type of negotiation focuses on the mutual and individual needs of both parties and their children, instead of delineating and staking out the exclusive and inflexible positions of the parties, as often happens in litigated divorces.

High conflict divorces, by their very nature, make avoiding stress much more difficult. Stress can lead to serious conditions such as depression, suppressed immune response, and poor decision making. Do your best to remain objective. Focusing on being calm, centered, and objective helps to reduce stress. Accept that the motives of your spouse may not be based on a win-win approach but a win-lose outcome. When faced with a spouse bent on seeing you "lose" and who has the means to see it through (either emotionally or financially), there is little incentive in trying to reason with your spouse, ask for fairness, or to offer concessions in the hope of creating a cooperative atmosphere. In fact, doing so could possibly escalate your spouse's demands and, consequently, create additional

stress for you. Work through your lawyer. Recognize and accept the means and motives of your spouse. Experienced Florida Board Marital and Family law attorneys are experts in navigating this divorce legal system, mitigating unreasonable demands, and will have the objectivity to formulate a plan, enjoin tactics, and drive forward to a settlement.

CONSIDER YOUR HEALTH

The mind/body connection is frequently discussed and much research points to the effects of mental stress on health. Now is the time to get serious about your health. A proper diet, moderate exercise, adequate sleep, and some counseling can have a very positive impact on your well-being and judgment. As with any change in your health regimen, we recommend that you consult with your doctor, and obtain his or her approval before you commence any exercise program or new diet. At the same time, you should consider obtaining a general medical evaluation of your health that you may have been putting off. Now is a good time to schedule it! Don't be afraid to consider seeking individual mental health counseling. Your lawyer will be more than happy to offer a referral. Keep in mind what is being suggested here is covered under most health plans. If you are covered, take advantage of those benefits.

At this moment, you may feel that you have your stress and health under control. Nevertheless, resist the temptation to put off creating a plan to manage your stress and maximize your health. Our experience has always been that stress levels during divorce can rapidly increase. A little planning in the beginning means that you will already have a routine established and a plan to maintain and manage your physical and emotional health.

Some people may feel uncomfortable about seeing a mental health professional. However, it is simple good advice. Even during the most amicable of divorces, a therapist can be the source of terrific insights and understanding that can be difficult to obtain from any other source. You might want to try more than one counselor, to locate a therapist who fits your personality. Therapists are aware that you need to find the right fit – discuss it with them.

DIET, SLEEP AND EXERCISE

Remember all of those things your mother told you when you were growing up? Eat a healthy diet; get plenty of sleep, and exercise. Well, mom was right. And while mom gave good advice, a lot of us have fallen into bad habits. Therefore, with the risk of sounding like your mother. Stay away from fat and sweets. Avoid fast food or other comfort foods and, especially avoid overeating. Use portion control. Overeating is a symptom of, and a response to stress. Unfortunately, the positive effects of overeating (gratification) are usually temporary and quickly may be replaced with guilt, less energy, and negative physical responses such as headaches. Instead, eat fruits, vegetables, and foods containing lean proteins. Drink plenty of water (avoid sodas, diet or otherwise) and stay hydrated.

Don't wear yourself out working on your divorce. Make sure you keep the late nights to a minimum and shoot for eight hours of sleep. A number of studies have demonstrated that eight hours of sleep is ideal to maintain peak performance and productivity. If the stress of the divorce makes it difficult to fall asleep, avoid regularly relying on pharmaceutical sleep-aids. Ask your doctor for a natural remedy or alternative. Moderate exercise is also the key to keeping a clear head. Recent studies suggest that spending time outdoors increases performance and creativity. Being here in Florida, gives you a distinct advantage with our many beaches and parks. Consider taking long walks on a beach or find some other way to take advantage of living in the "Sunshine State."

DOMESTIC VIOLENCE

The occurrence of domestic violence crosses all social, economic and racial boundaries. If you are the victim or the perpetrator of domestic violence, it is important to bring up the topic with your lawyer as early as possible. Fortunately, experienced family law attorneys are educated and experienced in domestic violence issues. They are quite familiar with the legal steps that should be taken, and sources of protection and help.

If you fear reprisal for filing for divorce, speak with an experienced Florida Board Certified Marital and Family Law attorney to ensure that you are properly protected. If you believe you or your children are in danger, you should find a safe place, and immediately contact the police and an attorney. If violence or a serious threat does occur, immediately dial 911 or contact the police immediately.

Florida currently has 42 domestic violence shelters. Help is available. For immediate assistance, call the Florida Domestic Violence Hotline at 1-800-500-1119 (TTY Hotline 1-800-621-4202).

CONSIDERATION 6: UNDERSTANDING THE COST OF DIVORCE

It is usually less expensive to obtain an uncontested divorce, since the need for legal work and advice may be considerably less. If you can't afford an attorney to represent you in your case, or if you have agreed on all of the issues with your spouse, you might consider the limited use (unbundled services) of an attorney to guide you procedurally and/or to review your paperwork prior to filing – the benefit you receive is legal advice and the assistance of the law firm for only the issues or legal work that you engage. In Florida, as in many states, the laws which circumscribe divorce, are often complex in how they may be applied from case to case. You can obtain a divorce, without the assistance of an attorney; however, the courts do not provide any different rules to you, then they do to attorneys, regarding the improper filing of documents and/or the application of Florida divorce law. Consequently, your attempts to complete your divorce yourself, could cause considerable delay and personal expense. The courts are themselves forbidden to provide legal advice, The Law Firm of Charles D. Jamieson, P.A., and other law firms in South Florida, offer unbundled services for individuals representing themselves (Pro Se Divorce), which can give you the benefit of properly filing court documents, enable you to meet requirements of Florida divorce laws, and save significant time, while avoiding unnecessary expense, and provide the benefit of the legal advice and assistance of a law firm.

Contested divorces, by their nature, are more expensive. Contested divorces require the building of a case (whether litigated in court or through a mediated settlement), most lawyers cannot do more than estimate what the total fees will be. In fact, the cost of the divorce will have as much to do with the position and emotional tone and responses of your spouse and his or her attorney as your own position.

Collaborative Divorce in Florida offers a less adversarial, less time consuming, and less expensive method for marriage dissolution. The Collaborative Divorce approach requires both parties and their individual attorneys to commit themselves to resolving all issues of the dispute by negotiated agreement. The parties and their lawyers enter into a legally binding contract not to resort to court for any reason except to introduce their Agreement into evidence and obtain a Final Judgment. The Collaborative process is applicable to all areas of Family Law.

The cost of divorce can be a shared expense between spouses. It is possible that a court may order one spouse to pay a portion of the other spouse's attorney fees for litigating or negotiating matters such as alimony, support, and timesharing/contact schedules.

LEGAL FEES

Most experienced family law attorneys (including those at our law firm) calculate legal fees on an hourly rate. Fees may be further broken down by lawyer, paralegal and other support staff. Many factors go into how much an individual lawyer. Specialization and length of practice often come into play and in Florida, the State Supreme Court directed The Florida Bar to offer a Board Certification Program for Florida attorneys. While any licensed lawyer may handle marital and family law matters at different levels, only those lawyers who have passed Board Certification are allowed by the Florida Bar to identify themselves as a specialist.

As a result, a lawyer's hourly rate can range dramatically. However, a higher hourly rate does not necessarily mean superior capabilities... be sure to ask your lawyer to explain his fees before agreeing to a retainer. Hourly rates in South Florida can generally range from $250 per hour and can exceed $500 per hour. Some law firms will offer flat fees. A flat fee may be charged for the entire divorce case or a specific/limited set of services. Unbundled services can also be offered to Pro Se litigants (where you represent yourself). In addition to a lawyer's legal fees, remember there are office expenses (postage, copying, faxing, and mileage), expert fees, court costs, and other expenses that may be involved in your case.

CONSIDERATION 7: FILING FOR DIVORCE

CHOOSING A GOOD DIVORCE LAWYER

As of June 2018, according to The Florida Bar, there are approximately 88,000 lawyers in Florida who are licensed by the Supreme Court of Florida to practice law in the State, only 269 of these attorneys are Board Certified Marital & Family Law Attorneys.

In Florida, Board Certification assists consumers in identifying specialists in various areas of law, including Marital and Family Law. The practice of Marital and Family Law is generally unique in the State of Florida, since decisional, statutory and procedural laws are specific to this State.

Board Certification is the highest level of evaluation by The Florida Bar of the competency and experience of attorneys in particular areas of law, including the area of Marital and Family Law. Board Certification recognizes an attorney's special knowledge, skills, and proficiency in an area of law, as well as professionalism and ethics in practice. Certified attorneys are the only lawyers allowed to identify or advertise themselves as "Florida Bar Board Certified," experts, or specialists.

Although there may be many excellent attorneys who are not Board Certified in Marital and Family Law, Board Certification by The Florida Bar clearly indicates that the attorney is specialized and has become an expert in the area of Marital and Family Law in Florida. In our law firm, Attorney Charles D. Jamieson and Doreen Inkeles are both Board Certified in Marital and Family Law.

If you would like some additional information on Board Certified Marital and Family Law Attorneys, The Florida Bar has published an article called, "Selecting an Attorney Specializing in Marital & Family Law." The Florida Bar also provides a directory of current Board Certified Marital and Family Law Attorneys by name and city.

INITIAL CONSULTATION

An initial consultation with a family law attorney is a very important consideration in planning your divorce. You will be depending heavily on your lawyer for knowledge and advice, and the attorney whom you choose to retain should be carefully vetted by you. The Florida Bar has made selecting an experienced attorney easier by certifying attorneys as specialists. Narrowing your search to a Florida Board Certified Marital and Family Law Attorney assures that the lawyer is committed to family law and has family law expertise. This is important because family law constantly changes and evolves – and it is difficult for a single lawyer to effectively practice law in multiple disciplines at the same time.

Your working relationship with your attorney is an important factor in your selection process. Consider why an attorney practices family law. Does the attorney hold the same or similar values as you? Many attorneys would make you think that it is about how many groups and organizations of which they are a member, or which law school they attended, and what newsletters they read. Board Certification means that you can be assured your attorney is up to date in their area of specialization, so focus instead on whether their values align with yours, or if they can accommodate your schedule, or if they will be able to effectively communicate with you. It is important that you find a lawyer who meets your expectations, make sure that you will be able to meet their expectations. So, ask the lawyer what they will expect from you as a client.

It is pretty simple… if you want to pursue an aggressive, adversarial strategy focused on preserving and protecting your assets and you are consulting with an attorney who is focused on equal parenting time and collaborative law approaches – well, you might not have a fit, at least not with the goals and values you want placed first.

Since Board Certified Marital and Family Law Attorneys invest a lot into obtaining and maintaining their specialization certification, they tend to be more expensive. Watch out for lawyers who are not certified but promise and overly promote low-cost divorces or "new cheap" approaches to divorce. You usually only get divorced once in your life and the results of your divorce can impact all aspects of your existence for the rest of your life. Helping to keep costs down is the goal of most experienced family law attorneys, but an attorney promoting the lowest cost can be a warning sign. Experienced family law attorneys have seen the devastating effects of these "low cost" divorces— often both spouses end up spending thousands more (at a later time) trying to correct what were ordinary, avoidable, mistakes.

The majority of family lawyers hold initial consultations in their offices. Some lawyers will offer more flexible approaches like a telephone consultation, online meetings and video teleconferencing.

A lot is dependent upon the law firm or lawyer's comfort level with today's technologies. Consider the convenience, money and time savings a lawyer is offering by being willing to have meetings on the phone or online. Adoption of modern technology also tends to reflect the efficiency and approach of the law firm in general. The flexibility they are exhibiting by offering both traditional and new methods of meeting is usually a good sign that they are seeking to minimize expenses, while maximizing their availability.

Do not expect initial consultations to be free, since many experienced family law attorneys require a fee for consultations. While some may not charge a fee, inquire with each law firm about what is covered during the initial consultation and what you can expect to walk away with beyond the discussion of a retainer. Remember, you usually get what you pay for.

Not all initial consultations will follow the same format and some lawyers may request that you have certain documents available for the initial consultation – so be sure to ask for guidelines from the lawyer or law firm to be prepared for the meeting. In general, it would be wise to have certain documents on hand during an initial consultation. You should consider bringing copies of at least the last two years of income tax returns and a prepared financial statement. Like many things, in life, your financial situation may dictate the best approach to your divorce since managing the expenses while securing your future will be a high priority.

Client and attorney relationships are unique. In fact, they are privileged relationships protected by law. Make the most of this relationship. Remember, arrive on time since it is courteous and shows respect. Work on building a level of trust immediately by being prepared with a list of questions specific to your case. Remain open and honest during your initial consultation so that the lawyer can give you an accurate assessment of your situation.

Your initial consultation with a lawyer should be an exchange. Your lawyer should be assertive but not overbearing. A lawyer should exhibit good listening skills and show patience in explaining complicated aspects of the law. If the lawyer you are meeting with leaves you confused or seems to be leading you – this is not a good sign. Trust your intuition… if you have any doubts, seek another opinion and meet with a different lawyer.

Also, let the lawyer interview you. The lawyer will be interested in the approach you want to take to pursue your divorce. Experienced and caring family law attorneys often operate on a set of principles and positions which they may have established about certain areas of family law.

Most experienced family law attorneys will talk about their principles and character on their websites. Family rights, the protection of children, equal parenting time, and other positions may be

important to the lawyer you are working with. Many lawyers look to align these values with their clients and avoid divorcing spouses who will use their children as pawns in "the fight," or those clients in general who are seeking to maliciously damage the other spouse.

ASK QUESTIONS AT THE INITIAL CONSULTATION

At the consultation, come prepared with a list of questions and, most importantly, ask to review the lawyer's written fee agreement:

Expenses:

What expenses do you charge for other than your time? How many of these expenses would you expect me to incur over the course of my divorce?

What types of expenses does the retainer cover? If there is a balance on the retainer, may I receive a refund?

Will I receive my charges in an itemized statement?

Do you have suggestions, or actions I can take to lower my costs?

Divorce Settlement:

Given what we have discussed about my case, what is a reasonable expectation for a settlement?

Do you foresee any serious challenges or setbacks with my case?

Do you know the judge likely to be assigned to my case and what do you think about them?

How flexible are your hours – do you ever work outside of normal business hours?

What do you feel is the best approach to my divorce – is collaborative divorce or an alternative dispute resolution process a good option for me?

Are you a Board Certified Marital and Family Law Attorney? If not, do you exclusively practice family law? If not, what percentage of your practice is focused on divorce or other family law issues?

Communications:

Can you explain how a call to your office is typically handled? What turnaround time should I expect if I leave a message?

Do you offer optional meetings online or through video teleconference? What equipment would I need to communicate with you?

How would you typically update me about developments in my case?

RATES AND RETAINERS

Prior to discussing rates and retainers you should have a very clear picture of how your lawyer will attempt to resolve your case. Generally, the options will be Pro Se or "tabletop" negotiations, mediation (with or without attorneys), collaborative divorce, and litigation. While no attorney can predict the future, experienced lawyers should be able to provide you with a reasonable timeframe and expectation for the outcome of your divorce. This assessment from the attorney is based on the outcomes of prior cases, similar negotiations, and their knowledge and experience gained from working within the local legal system.

During an initial consultation, your lawyer should be able to provide you with a thorough explanation of their billing and payment policies. Asking for a sample billing statement is often a good idea and can be used to discuss, in detail, how charges are detailed and billed. When you look at a billing statement, you should be able to clearly understand what work was performed and what length of time was required. The lawyer should be able to identify the hourly rates of the staff who will work on your case as well as projected expenses and how they will be shown on the billing statement. Learn which expenses will be passed through onto the billing statement, and which, if any expenses may be billed separately or by a third party. And, although we all generally understand what a "retainer" is – there are differences among attorneys in how retainers are used. Discuss with the lawyer how the retainer will be used and what services the retainer will or will not cover. Sometimes a portion or all of a retainer will be non-refundable – be sure to inquire how you are contractually obligated when paying your lawyer through a retainer.

Never agree to accept legal services if you feel you will not be able to pay for them. Failure to pay your legal bills could jeopardize the outcome of your divorce. Instead, work with your attorney to identify what you can pay, early and up front. You may be able to work with your attorney to identify potential future payment sources. This should be discussed up front and in the beginning of the divorce process.

Experienced attorneys usually are able to identify cases where they expect fees and costs to be high. Most often, fees and costs will be increased by the actions of an uncooperative spouse who is seeking to make the divorce process as painful and expensive as possible. Usually this means that the process of discovery will be costly since it will likely require a court's intervention and your lawyer's time to respond to issues, problems in the case and file motions. Other causes of expensive divorces may be the marital assets and liabilities themselves, since the estate may be financially complicated, or the assets are difficult to value (i.e. stock options, privately held businesses, etc.).

CONTROLLING COSTS

Believe it or not, the person with the most power to control the cost of your divorce is you! Keeping legal fees down means sharing your concerns with your lawyer up-front. Lawyers can typically off load some work and education assignments to their clients – but it is a balancing act, and it is critical that you complete assignments from your lawyer in a timely manner. When working with your lawyer, always assign tasks to yourself with an agreed upon deadline for completion. If you feel you are not up to the task, communicate that concern early with your lawyer – delays cost time, and time is the biggest expense in legal matters – whether the time is yours, the courts, or your lawyer's.

Organize your time to make some progress on your divorce each day. Divorce is work… treat it like you treat a job. Good *communication* with your lawyer is critical. Most experienced family law attorneys use case management software integrated with email – expect the majority of your communications and document exchanges to occur over email. This means you should be monitoring and organizing your email each day.

Work on *educating* yourself about divorce. Experienced family law attorneys provide education resources to their clients. Often clients are provided with references to books, articles and websites which will assist them in educating themselves about the legal issues in their case and with questions regarding non-legal issues; involving parenting during divorce, co-parenting with cooperative and uncooperative spouses, how to inform their children about the break-up or divorce between their parents, and other issues concerning individuals who are going through a divorce.

As a consequence, you can make educated decisions in a timely manner and conversations with your lawyer will be more efficient.

Next, *prioritize* the goals for your divorce with your lawyer. During the course of your divorce, your priorities may change, but prioritizing will allow your legal team to focus their efforts and your money on what is most important to you.

Finally, stay *involved*. At our law firm, we often urge clients to help us accumulate financial information regarding the history of their relationship and break-up. Doing so will reduce the amount in effort and time for attorneys and paralegals to obtain this information. This will also reduce the client's costs and helps clients feel more secure in their case.

OTHER COST CONTROL TIPS

Because the cost of divorce is so closely associated with the use of time – think about how your interactions with your lawyer and other family law professionals can be handled more efficiently and take less time to accomplish. By batching together your questions and comments, you can maximize the use of the time spent discussing those issues. Often questions or comments about your case do not need an immediate response. Instead, keep a journal and write down your questions and comments that can wait awhile before you have to discuss them with your attorney. Some people may be more comfortable using a smart-phone, computer or tablet to organize notes and questions. No matter how you approach it, collecting your questions and then addressing them at the one time with your lawyer, can save you legal fees. Batching your questions reduces interruptions, and the time otherwise taken up by responding to issues individually. Of course, there will be circumstances when you need an immediate answer. In those cases, indeed press for an answer. It is also important for you to understand the answers to your questions. Never give an indication you understand, if you do not. Misunderstandings can cause delays and backtracking. If you don't understand something, be clear with your lawyer about your lack of understanding before moving forward

The option of going to court is like the antidote for snakebite… if you get bit, you'll want to have access to the antidote. Of course, you should avoid going into the woods (where the snakes are located) in the first place. Pushing to go to court to resolve disputed issues should be the plan of last resort. For your lawyer, preparing for court (litigation) is often more expensive than actually litigating the issues in court. As a rule of thumb, it can take 2 to 5 days for every hour of hearings or trial, depending on the complexities of issues, to prepare. If you want to control costs, put your emotions in check and put them in your pocket with your pocketbook. While you may feel righteous and good to threaten your spouse with a date at the courthouse, this is usually an expensive

strategy. Threatening to go to court is likely to trigger a response from your spouse's lawyer – which may undermine or thwart the strategy your lawyer has been planning or trying to implement. Your lawyer will know when a threat to go to court is warranted. Learn to walk away from unmediated conversations with your spouse that can turn argumentative. Controlling costs also is about having a strategic plan with your lawyer. Working the game plan requires that you practice the four key points made on the previous page: Communication, Education, Prioritization, and Involvement.

If you are working a strategic plan with your lawyer, you will be less likely to fall into another expensive trap – letting your spouse's lawyer do all the work. Your spouse's lawyer has no requirement to protect your interests, and while it is unlikely they will maliciously pursue you, every step in the divorce process presents subtle choices that can help or hurt you in the future. And remember, the final distribution of assets is final. Engaging in a working strategy with your lawyer will mean that you can frame the issues you face instead of being on a defensive posture, where your lawyer is merely reacting to your spouse's attorney.

IDENTIFY YOUR TEAM AND DOCUMENTS

Choosing a family lawyer to work with is first and foremost. And, even if you feel you can go through the divorce process on your own (Pro Se) – having sat down with and discussed your pending divorce with a lawyer is a valuable experience in terms of creating a realistic expectation of what lies ahead, and also in terms of identifying possible experts who may be warranted by your circumstances and resources. You may not need to work with any professionals, or you may need to consult or work with more than one. As you develop your case and strategy with your lawyer, discuss what additional advisors or experts you may need. Your lawyer is going to be your best source for referrals – they should be aware of which advisors or experts are best matched to you, your needs, and whether they have a good professional working relationship with your attorney.

In many divorces, the help of a mental health professional is important in assisting you with the emotional aspects of divorce. They can help to recognize and minimize (or avoid) bouts of depression, and provide the coaching needed to get through the tough emotional times ahead. Forensic psychologists can assist with mental health issues involved in timesharing and contact schedules with your children. Financial advisors are instrumental where detailed budgets are required and can help to accurately project and justify your future financial needs. There are other financial experts that may be necessary to identify, classify, and value marital property subject to division, like forensic accountants. When a family business is involved, it may require a business appraiser to determine its worth. A vocational expert may be needed to evaluate the earning capacity of spouses, and project earnings after additional education or retraining.

Thinking about the range of experts who may be required during a divorce, may seem a little daunting. But remember this will be a process that occurs in a series of steps. When you get to the various bridges you need to cross, don't hesitate to engage an expert when it is warranted. Also, keep in mind that you too will become a bit of an expert in your own right. Take notes at meetings, build upon your knowledge, and many of your concerns will diminish as your attorney develops and implements with you the game plan to obtain your goals.

Early on, your lawyer will give you a very detailed list of documents and information necessary for your case. The sooner the information and documents can be assembled and secured the better. Don't count on the records being available at a later time. Paper documents can become lost or damaged – make copies of important documents as soon as possible. Electronic records are usually available for download as pdf files. You can also use screen capture software to create documentation of certain records like a drill down of a checking account, when a pdf version is not readily available. The best option is to store all of the documentation with your lawyer – for safekeeping. This is an important first step and will make it difficult for the other spouse to hide assets or income at a later time.

PETITION FOR DIVORCE

In Florida, you file a Petition for Dissolution of Marriage to start the legal process of divorce. The "petition for divorce" and claims for relief included therein, generally ask the court to order alimony, child support, timesharing, contact schedules, the division of assets and liabilities, attorneys' fees, and all other relevant claims or demands for relief. If a claim for relief is not contained in the initial pleading, relief cannot be granted. Thus, a complaint for divorce that asks for everything may be used as a means to preserve your claims. In a similar fashion, if you are the respondent to a Petition for Dissolution of Marriage, your Counter Petition should ask for everything possible, to preserve your claims to the same at trial.

To file a Petition for Dissolution of Marriage in Florida, you must have been a resident of Florida for the six-month period immediately preceding the filing of the petition for divorce. If you are temporarily living out of state, the judge will need to determine whether or not you are still a Florida resident or domiciled in Florida. This usually is based on what the judge considers your intent to be (based on a number of different factors) If the court believes you have no intention to return, the judge may consider you not to be a resident and ineligible to file for divorce. Florida residents who are members of the military, but who are stationed out of state or overseas are not affected. In matters concerning the custodial care of children, courts often look at where the children have lived for the prior six months to determine initial jurisdiction. Most states have adopted a law called the Uniform Child Custody Jurisdiction and Enforcement Act (UCCJEA); even so, divorces involving jurisdictional issues can be complicated, which adds to their expense. A Petition for Dissolution of Marriage is most often filed in the county where the spouses last lived together. If neither spouse is still living in that county, the case will most likely be filed in the county where the petitioner (filing spouse) lives at the time.

After it is filed with the court, a summons and the Petition for Dissolution of Marriage and other documents must be served upon the petitioner's spouse (the respondent). If you know where your spouse lives, you should use a personal service. The person who delivers the notice must be a process server or a deputy sheriff. In cases where your spouse is out of state, you would still use a personal service to provide notice of the petition through a legal process served in your spouse's location. In the event the whereabouts of the spouse is unknown or if your spouse is out of the country, you may use constructive service. Additionally, if your spouse is in the military service of the United States, additional steps may be required. When a spouse cannot be serviced, an Affidavit of Diligent Search and Inquiry is required. The law regarding constructive service is complex and you may want to consult with an attorney to make sure you fulfill the requirements of the law. When constructive service is used, other than granting a divorce, the relief which you may obtain may be limited.

WHO FILES FIRST?

Usually, there is little advantage to who files first since most divorce cases settle before going to trial. However, if there is a trial, it is likely that the party that files first will get to argue first, and this is considered a strategic advantage. In some instances where spouses are already living separately (separate counties or states), then whoever files first has the benefit of selecting the venue. In some instances, the party filing first is simply more committed to obtaining a divorce. If you know you will pursue temporary support and/or a mandatory injunction, it is to your benefit to file first, since you must file for divorce prior to requesting a temporary relief hearing.

TEMPORARY SUPPORT

Temporary support may be awarded after a petition for divorce has been filed and if the spouses cannot reach an agreement regarding how to handle their bills and finances. Florida courts recognize discrepancies in the incomes of spouses and provides access to temporary support through the filing of a Motion for Temporary Relief. Temporary support can be comprised of temporary alimony, child support, and attorney's fees. In Florida, the trial judge will hear the motion. A Motion for Temporary Relief is heard in an abbreviated (short) hearing – the courts are not interested in a long, drawn-out temporary relief hearing and often place time limitations on the proceedings. Testimony will involve financial issues including income, debts, and bills. However, issues concerning timesharing (custody and visitation) and other issues concerning the children will also be heard. During the process of divorce, the courts will try to ensure that the financial status quo is maintained until a final divorce resolution is reached. And just because one spouse may be required to pay a certain amount in temporary support, the final amount of ongoing spousal support/alimony, is not determined until the final judgment for divorce is entered and the temporary order ends.

An important point to remember about temporary support issues is that either spouse (petitioner or respondent) may initiate and file a Motion with the court requiring temporary relief. The court itself will not automatically make temporary support "a part of the process," although there are stages where the court may inquire about the status of the case, the court is more concerned about the progress towards reaching a final settlement or if the case will be going to trial.

INJUNCTION

Another form of temporary relief is an injunction. Florida law provides either party (petitioner or respondent) the ability to obtain a court order preventing either spouse from engaging in certain potentially harmful activities, including: the disposal of marital property, cancellation of life insurance policies, harassment at a workplace, confrontations in the presence of children, destruction of records, removal of children from a school, taking children out-of-state, and can require children's passports to be held in an escrow account. Again, obtaining injunctions is a complex process. You should consult with an attorney to advise you.

THE COST TO FILE

The cost of filing a petition for divorce in Florida depends on the county. Some counties are more expensive than others. In Palm Beach County, Florida, the cost may be over $409.

To file for divorce in Florida, fees must be paid when you file the petition for divorce at your county courthouse. The petitioner will be the one to pay the court fees for filing a Petition for Dissolution of Marriage. However, the respondent will pay a fee when they file a Counter-Petition.

Most Circuits in Florida require that spouses attend mediation before having a temporary relief hearing or the final hearing – if the mediation is unsuccessful, the parties can pursue their case through the courts. An accepted alternative to court ordered mediation is participation in a collaborative law process. The key of either process resulting in a settlement depends on the willingness of both parties to timely share the entirety of the needed financial information and a willingness to cooperate. Most cases will eventually settle even if, the divorce is litigated. Litigation is prohibitively expensive, public, and can drag out over a long period of time, making settlement a more attractive option as both spouses approach the date scheduled for the Final Hearing or Trial of their divorce.

CONSIDERATION 8: WHY YOU SHOULD CONSIDER GETTING DIVORCED IN 2018

The 2018 Federal Tax Bill abolished alimony deductions – and will make divorces after January 1, 2019 much more difficult to resolve.

Most of us are aware of the Tax Cuts and Jobs Act passed by the Federal Government in January, 2018. What most of us do not realize is that under the new tax bill, newly divorcing spouses have until December 31, 2018, to obtain a Final Judgment in their divorce case in Florida or they will lose the tax deduction that they could receive for paying alimony.

All divorces that have been concluded by Final Judgment in the State of Florida prior to January 1, 2019, will still be able to deduct their alimony payments. In essence, tax-deductible alimony for those divorces will be "grandfathered in." However, all divorces concluded on or after January 1, 2019, will lose the ability to deduct alimony payments.

This change in the tax code can have a catastrophic impact on divorces. Payors of alimony and recipients of alimony may lose tens of thousands, if not hundreds of thousands, of dollars from the loss of deduction in alimony payments.

Divorce lawyers are predicting that the loss of alimony deductibility will make divorces more difficult to resolve and will have a negative financial impact on all divorces. Spouses often face starkly different pictures in terms of their post-divorce financial stability and lifestyles. Although alimony is often a contentious issue, eliminating the tax deduction will not eliminate alimony itself. Instead, it will limit the ability of judges, attorneys, and parties to find common ground in divorce cases by maximizing each other's post-divorce financial position. Without the additional flexibility of alimony deduction, alimony and divorces in general, will become more of a zero-sum game in which one party "wins" and the other party "loses." Eliminating the tax deduction will not eliminate alimony. It will just make the already strained Family Court System less efficient, reduce total family income, making divorce negotiations more difficult. In Florida, alimony is not limited to the wealthy; it is a tool that can be used by the Court to ensure that former spouses stay above the poverty line.

Alimony has been one of the few systemic antidotes to a modern demographic trend by providing financial protection for spouses who choose to rear children instead of choosing professional advancement. Alimony reduces the risk for spouses who focus on family rather than career. Over the long run, weakening alimony is likely to hasten the current trend away from child-rearing and towards a society in which both spouses focus on their respective careers—or face financial calamity if their marriage ends. Those who wish for a return to the "good old days" in America—where the husband worked and the mother stayed home to tend to the children—should remember that in modern America, the wife would have very little incentive to stay home with the kids if a future divorce means financial destruction. If alimony becomes more limited (because of its lost deductibility), sacrificing one's career to raise children and support a spouse becomes a grievous proposition. With no alimony safety net, spouses who fail to earn during the marriage could be left destitute after a divorce. The loss of alimony deductibility also means less money for divorced families. Historically, alimony has allowed individuals to give and receive financial support in a way that maximizes tax savings for the family. For alimony payors—who must sacrifice a significant part of their earnings to a former spouse—the deduction reduced the financial burden of spousal support. That was because all alimony paid would be deductible against income, dollar-for-dollar. If you were in the 40-percent bracket and paid $10,000 a month in alimony, you could use all $10,000 to deduct against your income. This meant that the $4,000 you would usually pay in taxes, you could save. Consequently, you would be spending in reality $6,000 to pay your spouse $10,000 (because you were saving $4,000 in tax payments). For recipients, the deduction permitted former spouses to receive larger amounts of support where recipients generally operate at lower tax brackets than alimony payors. The loss of deductibility means the loss of the additional alimony to the less affluent spouse. Obviously, over a course of a post-divorce relationship the loss of alimony deductibility, could cost both the potential payor and recipient of alimony tens of thousands, if not hundreds of thousands of dollars.

It will make it far more difficult for attorneys to negotiate reasonable and necessary alimony or spousal support payments in their divorce cases. After December 31, 2018, spouses will be paying dollar for dollar to ex-spouses and not getting any tax relief. Paying spouses will not receive any tax relief from deducting their alimony payments, they will be less likely and willing to pay as much in alimony.

Many individuals and attorneys also have failed to realize that the removal of alimony deduction in divorce cases commencing January 1, 2019, runs headlong into the problem of the congestion of the court dockets in family courts in Florida and across the country. Currently in Palm Beach County, depending on the judge before whom you are appearing, it may take 9 to 12 or more months to process a standard litigated divorce; in other words, a divorce that may have one or two small issues that need to be litigated and resolved at a final hearing before a judge. For cases that have many complex issues to be resolved; it will take far more than 12 months to finalize the divorce. Consequently, individuals who have doubts about the stability of their marriage, individuals who are contemplating ending their marriage, and individuals who are in the middle of a divorce which is not going anywhere, need to understand that they are at risk of losing the protection and benefits of deductibility of alimony. These individuals must consult with an experienced family law attorney in order to develop a strategy to assess whether they should proceed with a divorce this year and if so, how they may ensure that they will achieve the protection of the deductibility of alimony in their case. Failure to do so may cost divorcing couples tens of thousands, if not hundreds of thousands, of dollars over the course of their lives long after the marriage has concluded by divorce. This is a serious problem and cannot be ignored. Your marriage may be absolutely solid; however, our office is confident that you know of people having problems in their marriage and may be contemplating divorce, or you know people who have commenced their divorce, but it is stagnant or is not moving forward quickly. You should determine if they are aware that the deductibility of alimony ends on December 31, 2018, and the impact it may have on their case. These people also should be seeking out the services of an experienced, Florida Board Certified Family Law attorney. Failure to do so may have devastating financial consequences to them and to their future.

CONSIDERATION 9: COLLABORATIVE DIVORCE

Collaborative divorce is an alternative to litigating a Dissolution of Marriage. It is also an alternative to ensure that you will conclude your divorce prior to January 1, 2019 and retain the advantage of deductibility of alimony. Collaborative divorce is a process whereby you and your spouse and each of your attorneys work with an independent, objective, financial professional and facilitator (most usually a mental health professional). Together, functioning as a team, they provide alternative solutions for the divorcing spouses to consider in formulating a result that meets the majority of both of their needs and the best interest of your children.

The parties and their attorneys sign a participation agreement. A participation agreement contains several critical clauses including, but not limited to:

1) The parties will be civil to one another throughout the process.

2) There will be full transparency regarding all issues in the case. This means that both parties will voluntarily, or at the request of a neutral financial professional, provide any and all financial documents or other information necessary for the financial professional to analyze the parties' financial status and to start fashioning alternatives for the parties to consider regarding the division of the marital assets, liabilities, alimony, and child support.

3) The parties will not take advantage of each other and immediately notify all participants when the other party has made a mistake or error and will not take advantage of any mistakes or errors they discover.

4) In the event that either party terminates the collaborative process to litigate their case in court, then the two attorneys are disqualified, the attorneys' law firms are disqualified, and the prior agreement of the parties to the neutral financial professional may also be disqualified. This disqualification process is important because it requires all participants to have "skin in the game." The attorneys no longer have the default of litigation if they can't resolve any issue. Consequently, they must become creative problem solvers on the issues that may develop during the collaborative process. In addition, as the fees for the professionals involved the case are paid, the parties will have more financial investment, and will be reluctant to abandon to process.

A series of private confidential meetings occur; prior to each meeting the parties trade agendas of the issues or items to be discussed or resolved so that there is no "ambushing" of one party by another during the meeting. If any new issues arise during the meeting, they are tabled, to be resolved at the next meeting.

The foundation of the collaborative process is set in place at the first meeting. The agenda of the first meeting is essentially to establish the rights and responsibilities of the parties, (i.e. who lives where, who drives what car, how are the bills going to get paid.) After a series of 2 to 4 meetings, generally most collaborative cases have resolved.

The collaborative process has its draw-backs, but it is faster than the normal litigation process (meaning that couples, who decide to get divorced later in the year 2018, may still be able to complete their divorce and obtain a Final Judgment before the January 1, 2019, deadline when all alimony deductibility will vanish or disappear).

The following are some additional benefits to be gained through the collaborative divorce process:

1) A collaborative divorce is less expensive than litigating a divorce. During litigation, experts are hired for both sides. Litigation also requires additional attorney fees taking depositions and filing discovery requests, all of which are very time consuming and can become very expensive. The often-prohibitive expense of litigating a divorce is reason enough to proceed with the collaborative divorce process.

2) You keep control of the outcome. When you decide to litigate a divorce, you are appearing in front of a judge. You are therefore putting the future of both of your lives and your children's future, in the hands of a stranger. Most divorce judges will tell you that they will attempt to do their best in every case; however, they also will admit they probably "will get it wrong." The people who know the most about the needs and the best interests of their children are the divorcing parents. The parties who know more about their marital assets and liabilities and the history of the marriage are the divorcing spouses. The discretion of a judge in making decisions in a divorce case is limited by Florida Statutes and Case Law. In a collaborative law case, the divorcing spouses are free to use creative "outside the box" options which fit their needs and the best interest of their children. Their discretion is only limited by their creativity.

3) You learn to communicate in a civil fashion and preserve a civil relationship that carries on with you, after the divorce is completed. This prevents the well-known dynamic of warring parents and their families sitting like two armed cats at the future major events of their children (graduations, marriage, christenings, etc.).

4) It is private and confidential. When you litigate your case, the public is permitted to be in the courtroom to watch any of the hearings that occur in your case. Any documents you file with the court, including financial documents, are available to be reviewed by the public. Consequently, collaborative divorce provides you anonymity, privacy and confidentiality which is not possible in a judicially litigated divorce proceeding.

5) You have a team working for you to create alternatives that meet the majority of the needs of both parties and each of their children.

The State of Florida recognized collaborative divorce by enacting the collaborative divorce statutes §61.55 through §61.58. Those statutes went into effect on July 30, 2017. The Florida Supreme Court has enacted rules of procedure regarding collaborative divorce. Together the collaborative divorce statutes and rules of procedure incorporate into law the components which I have outlined in this book.

Because it is faster, private, and less expensive, collaborative divorce is a viable alternative to the majority of people considering divorce. Those individuals who wish to ensure that they retain the deductibility of alimony in their divorce cases should consider collaborative divorce an essential, if not necessary, method of finalizing their divorce as the year 2018 progresses. This alternative is potentially the only way the divorcing parties may avoid having their cases slowed by congestions of the court system and be able to successfully move their divorce to Final Judgment before January 1, 2019.

Charles D. Jamieson has participated in introductory and advanced collaborative law training courses. He has been participating in collaborative divorce cases for over 15 years. If you are interested in proceeding with a collaborative divorce, contact our office and schedule a consultation. It will be well worth the money you spend. To learn more information about collaborative divorce, please visit our blog at www.cjamiesonlaw.com and our YouTube channel at Charles D. Jamieson P.A. https://www.youtube.com/channel/.

WHAT'S NEXT

"Don't wait. The time will never be just right. Stop where you stand and work with whatever tools you may have at your command and better tools will be found as you go along." —Napoleon Hill.

So, you've read the book, at the very least you flip to the end of the book to see what wisdom may be contained at that point in the book. If you're reading this book in 2018 then you have little time to waste. The revocation of the deductibility of alimony is an important issue that you must weigh regarding when to you start your divorce. Commencing a divorce and ending a relationship is not an easy step to take. The future result of a divorce is unknown. It is normal to fear the unknown and to fear the emotional pain and financial uncertainty that a divorce may bring. At the same time, working with an experienced Board-Certified Family Law Attorney will make that uncertain journey much easier. If, at this point in time, you're still uncertain as to whether or not you should file a divorce or to eliminate some of the uncertainty about commencing such a monumental change in your life, you can contact our office and schedule a consultation. We guarantee that you'll obtain valuable information and will leave the consultation more knowledgeable, calmer, and with a better understanding of the next step you should take. You will find that it will be the best money that you've spent in a long time. So, make the call, and schedule a consultation. We look forward to meeting you and working with you.

"You don't have to see the whole staircase, just take the first step." —Martin Luther King.

Read this entire e-book. The book was designed to describe the first set of considerations that you may face when going through a divorce in Florida. From here, you will be able to start organizing yourself and prepare the right questions to ask an experienced attorney. With the answers to those questions, you can make better decisions. We believe in a set of guiding principles. This book was organized around our guiding principles: Communication, Education, Prioritization, and Involvement. You can learn more about our guiding principles by going to our website here. Remember that there are always exceptions and your case could be different than what is described here. The content in this e-book is for informational purposes only and should not be construed as legal advice on any subject and is not intended as legal advice on your particular case. You should always consult with your own attorney before implementing anything you read or hear on the internet. The content of this e-book/book does not create any legal relationship between you and Charles D. Jamieson, Esquire or The Law Firm of Charles D. Jamieson, P.A. or any of its attorneys. All this having been said, I hope you enjoyed this book.

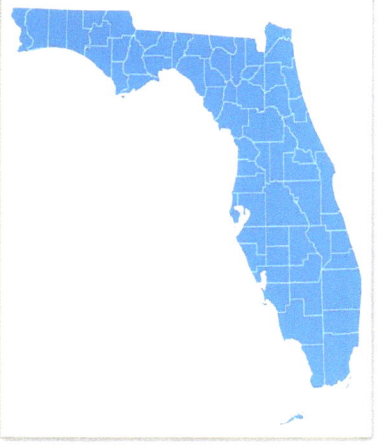

www.ingramcontent.com/pod-product-compliance
Lightning Source LLC
Chambersburg PA
CBHW040411220526
45473CB00004B/1203